Holy Shit

Adult Swear Word Coloring Book

For Stress Relief

By

S.B. Nozaz

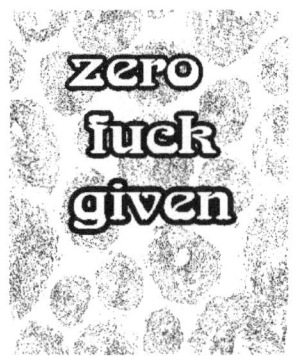

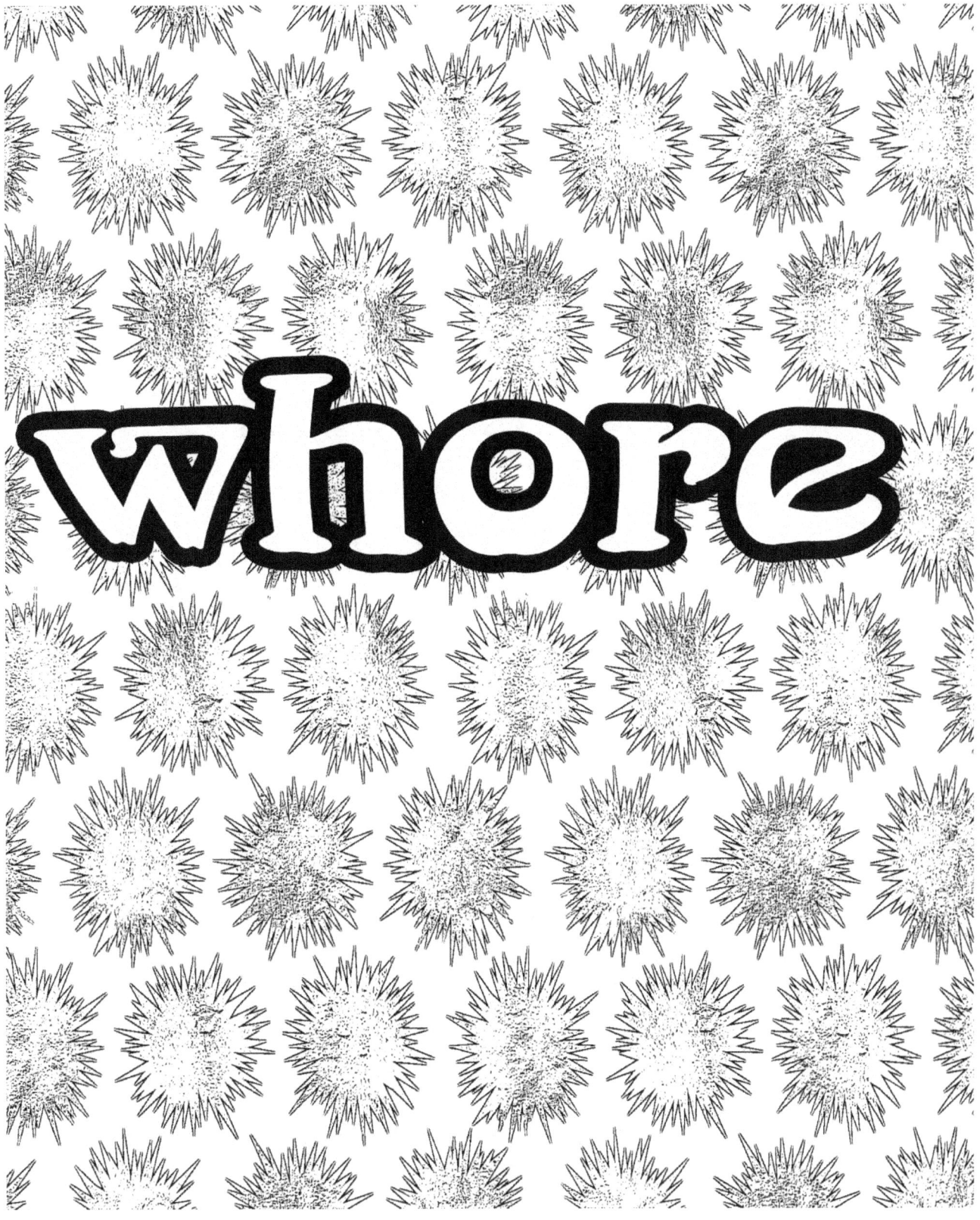

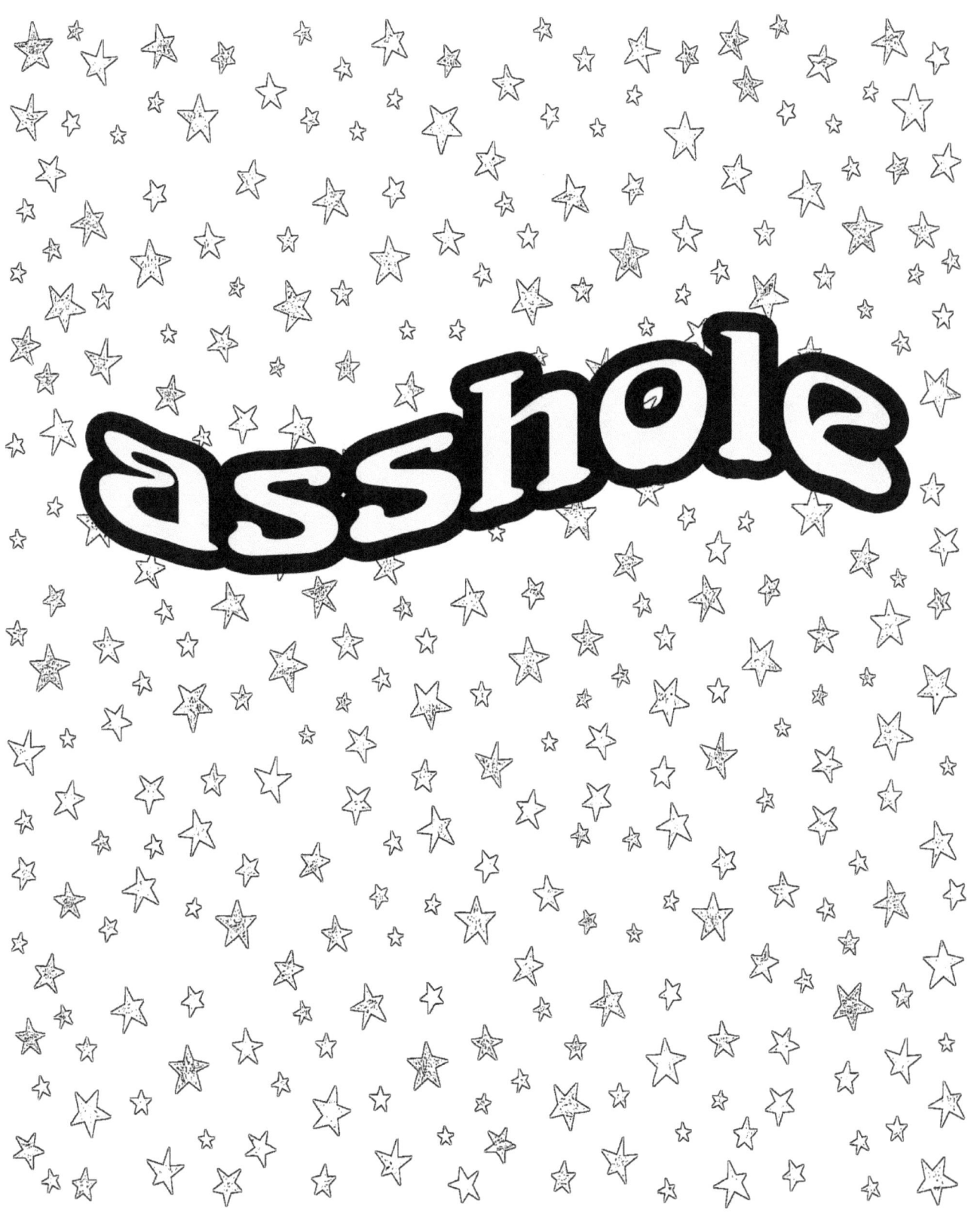

batshit

crazy

attention

whore

fuck

a

duck

kiss

my

ass

cuntface

cock

and

balls

bastard

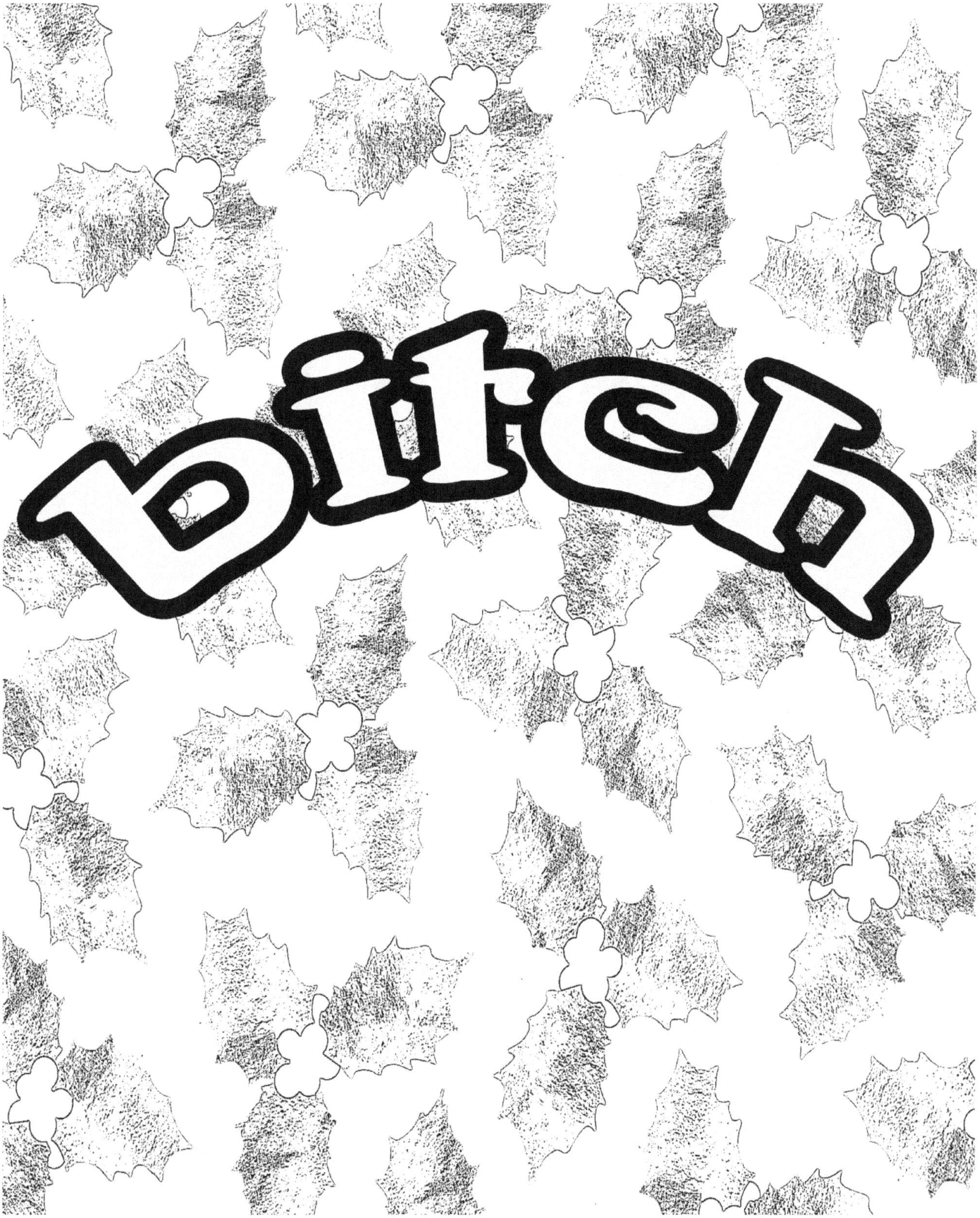
bitch

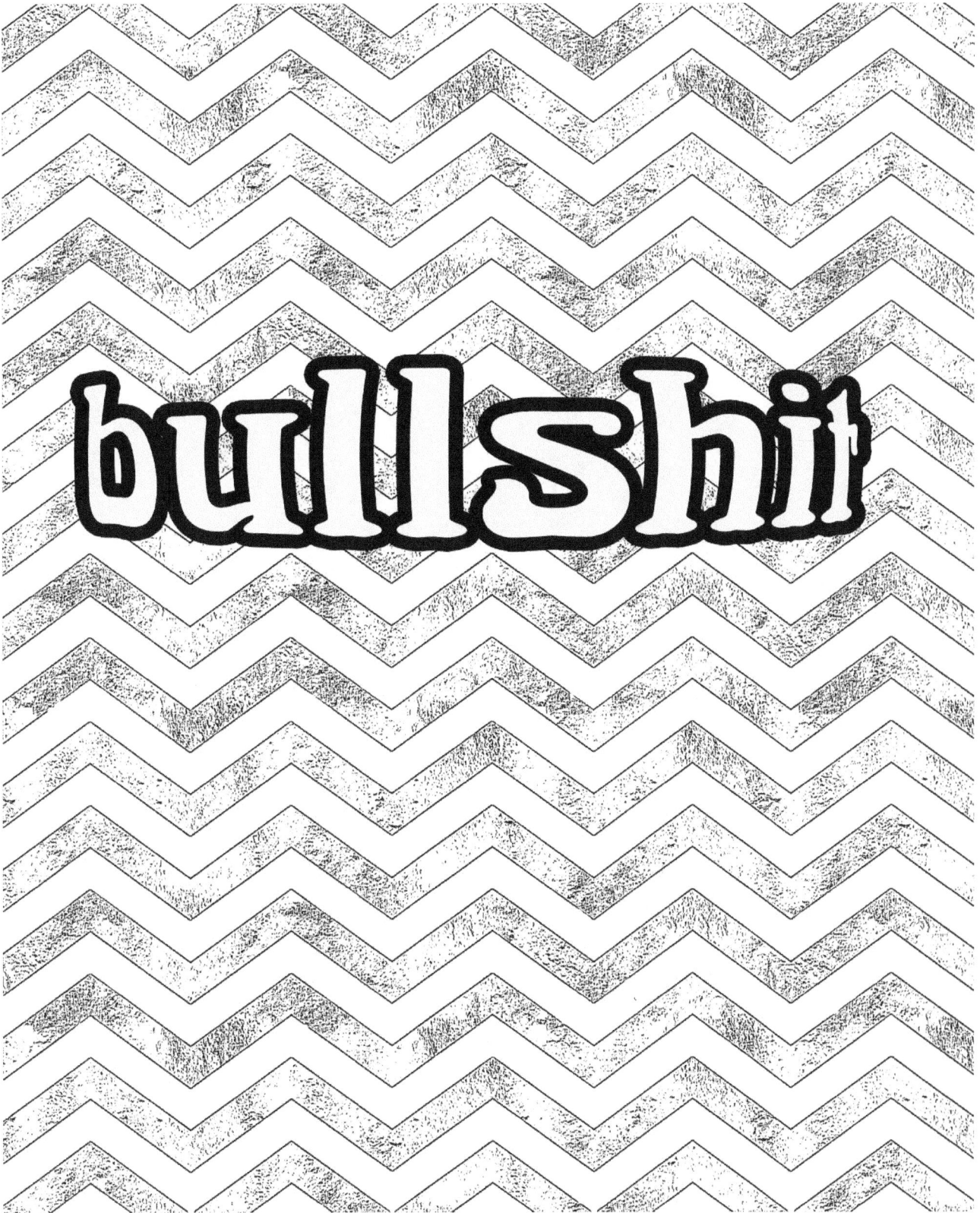

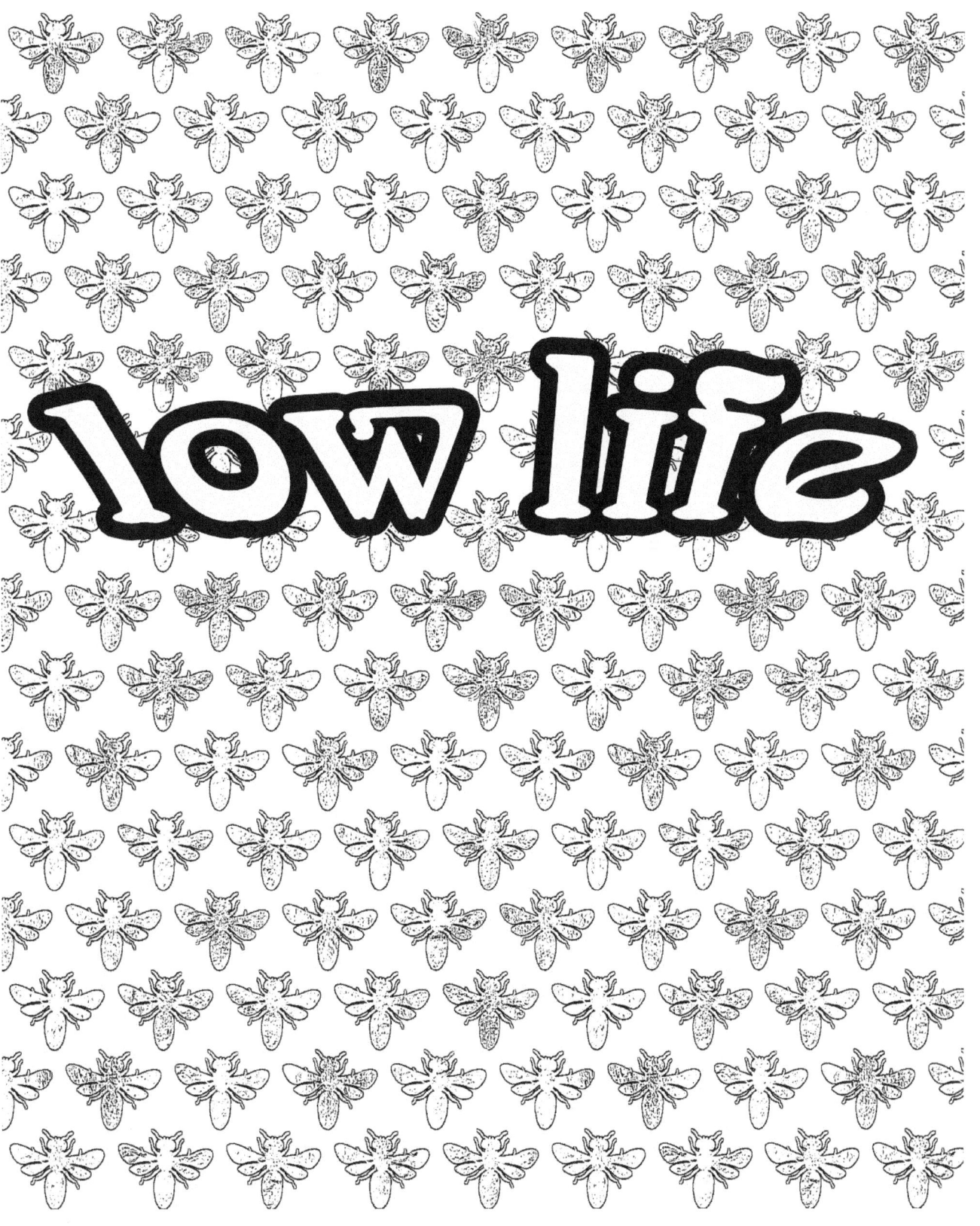

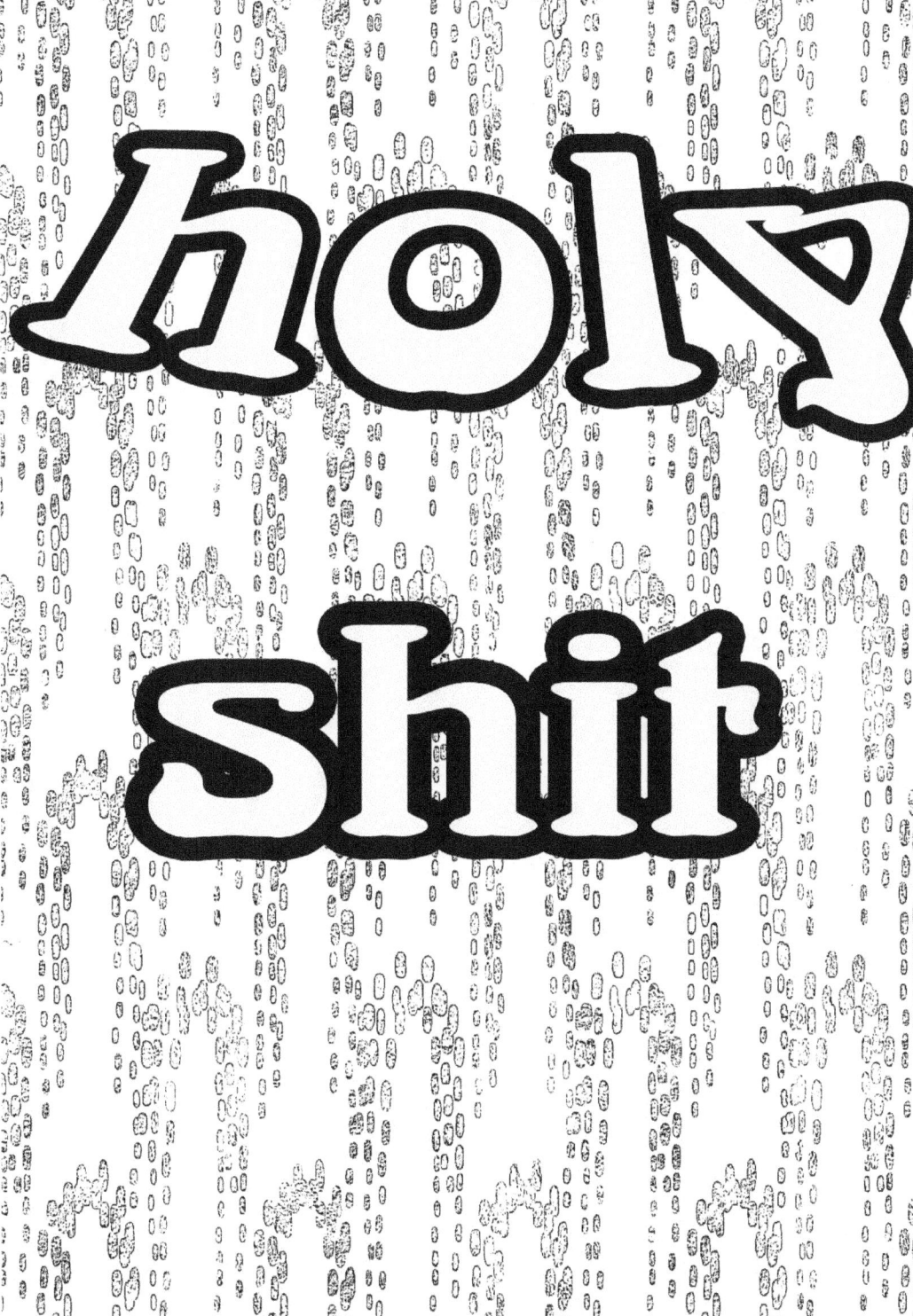

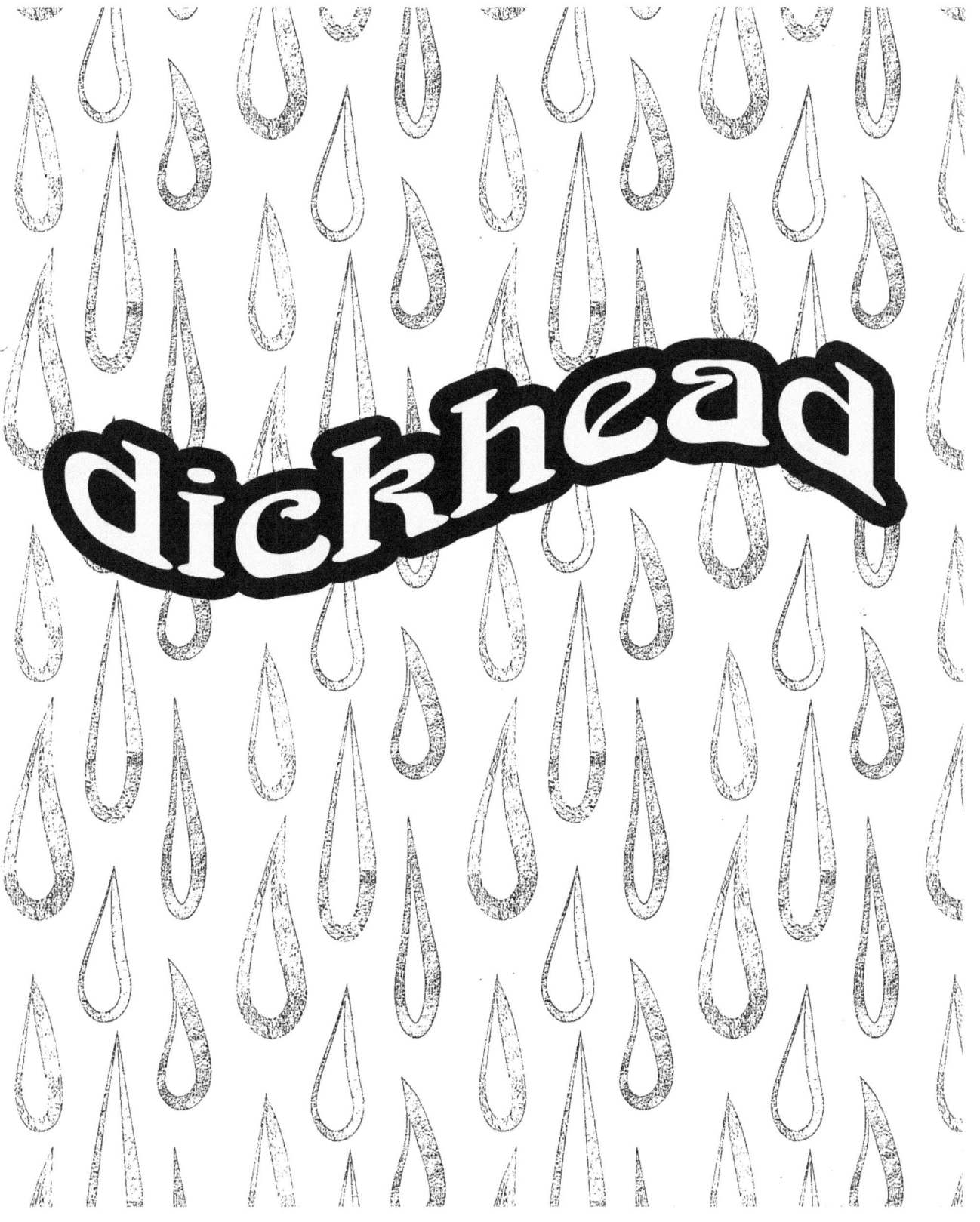

zero fuck given

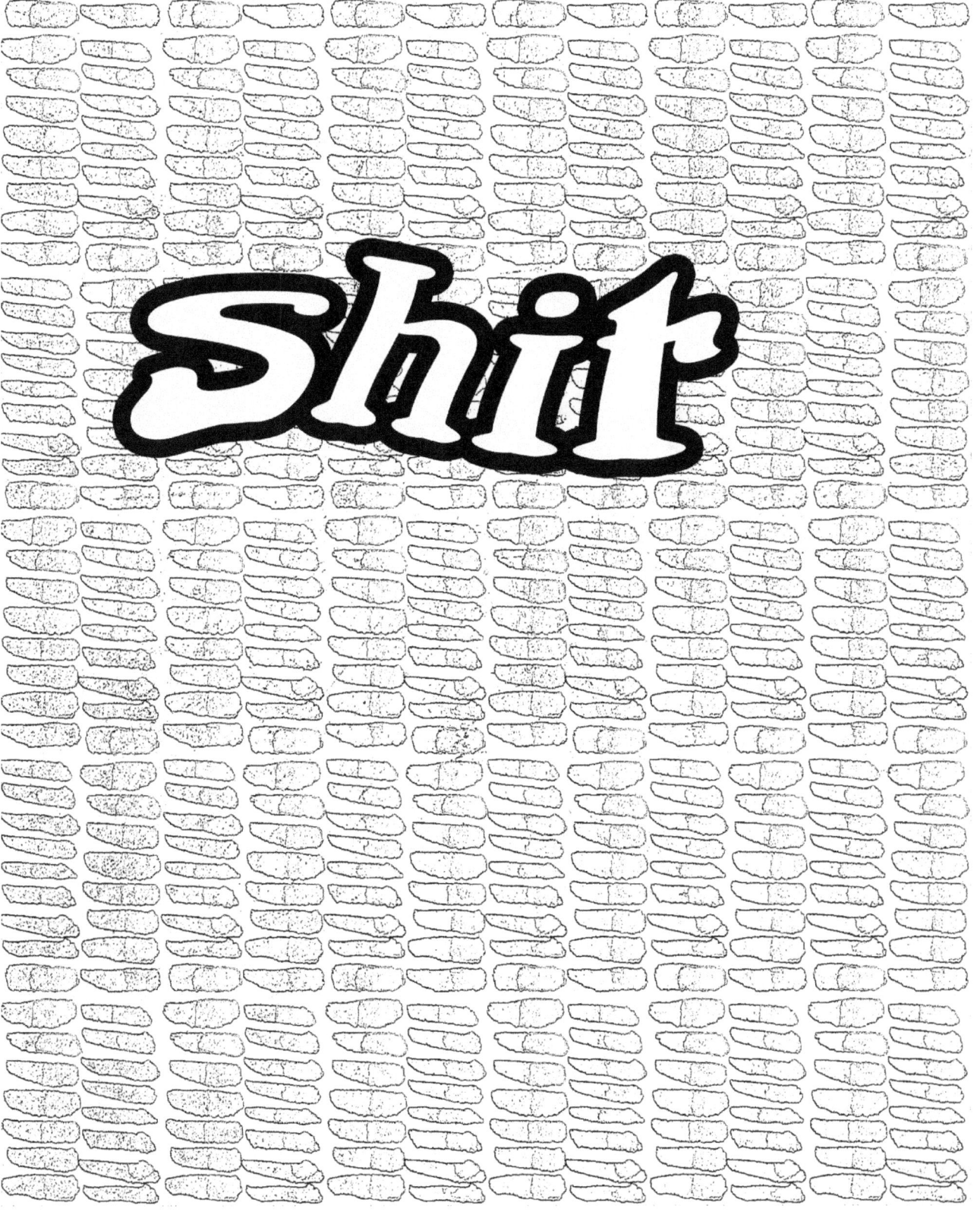

Note

www.ingramcontent.com/pod-product-compliance
Lightning Source LLC
Chambersburg PA
CBHW080644190526
45169CB00009B/3499